GRACE ENGINE

JOSHUA BURTON

The University of Wisconsin Press

Publication of this book has been made possible, in part, through support from the Brittingham Trust.

The University of Wisconsin Press
728 State Street, Suite 443
Madison, Wisconsin 53706
uwpress.wisc.edu

Gray's Inn House, 127 Clerkenwell Road
London EC1R 5DB, United Kingdom
eurospanbookstore.com

Printed in the United States of America
This book may be available in a digital edition.

Library of Congress Cataloging-in-Publication Data

Names: Burton, Joshua (Poet), author.
Title: Grace engine / Joshua Burton.
Other titles: Wisconsin poetry series.
Description: Madison, Wisconsin : The University of Wisconsin Press, [2023]
  | Series: Wisconsin poetry series
Identifiers: LCCN 2022028834 | ISBN 9780299341640 (paperback)
Subjects: LCGFT: Poetry.
Classification: LCC PS3602.U769775 G73 2023 | DDC 811/.6—dc23/eng/20220819
LC record available at https://lccn.loc.gov/2022028834

GRACE ENGINE

WISCONSIN POETRY SERIES

Sean Bishop and Jesse Lee Kercheval, series editors
Ronald Wallace, founding series editor

for us

Do not speak to me of martyrdom . . .
—SONIA SANCHEZ

I am in danger. You are in danger.
—ADRIENNE RICH

Contents

I

The Hearing We Inherit

I cannot manage language, but my body
still has more options than to listen—

    two men crying in a green truck,
    the house of the slowly given up.

Prayer and periphery both share
the same rhythm—

    I once knew a red-haired white woman
    suffering from the disease of killing
    herself.

    At the white woman's wake,
    a poet with my name read Hoagland's poem
    "Suicide Song" and it made me sick.

In my father's cruelty, he named me *Yeshua*.
A name that carries with it the brutality of a brickbat.

And yes, *Joshua*, you lost your mind again
yesterday—

    like how the housewife left her key in the door—

and yes, it is all yours—
the steer and smear
of letting someone in.

I've been having
a different relationship
with ghosts—

They came to me
and quiet all night.
Said nothing.
But expected
something
of me.

They rarely came to us
as children, back when
I was at the age
when Aunt Brenda
called us *nigglets*.

Back when an older cousin
would tease a younger cousin,
calling her names synonymous
with darkness, like

Midnight,
   Hershey, &
      Shadow.

The ghosts watched us
with tenderness,
as to not wake us.

On one occasion, I mimicked him
calling the younger cousin Black in insult.

The look of betrayal on her face.

And this was when I learned metaphor.
How I must have seen her hue as see-through.

Years later, I heard that the older cousin
tried to set a white woman on fire.

My cousins, I still love them
like I love the night.

    How we are there,
    and not there.

If I could name myself,
it would be *Wisteria*.
The sky's fissure—

    We heard stories
    of our grandmother
    in her cabin house
    shooting away
    a black bear.

Now, the ghosts come to me
in threes.

They say the price of admission
is juxtaposition and three forms
of forgiveness.

In *black* and *gray* and *red*.

    I say,

I love you all, and love you and love you
and love you

    but my hands still shake in June.

Grace & Pity

for Sue

I was a too-religious child,
unsubtle in the way I spoke:

a cistern with a broken ladder inside, a month
    from one voice to the next.

    Bible in backpack, Bible in pillowcase, ichthys
to chest, over the shirt.

I would spend all my days like this.

When I used to hear God,
        it sounded like the making-
love of monkeys.

A bed is now my grandmother's only home.
She only looks
   past me.
We burned through religion like a robe.

      I tell her
to stop trying to take off her clothes
to free herself from the wires,

I tell her to stop trying
to remove her left-hand control mitt.

She is civil as two sons
sitting on a park bench.

Her will to live is like my will for muteness.

And yet we hear the same
departure.

The thick wrist of the storm
strangling Memorial Hermann Hospital
is music. The hanging-

wall quilt with the picture of Jesus
and lambs in her old apartment
blistered my back when I leaned against it.

    I turned my fear and anger toward it.

To me, God's face would look like a lesula,
long-faced and ancestral like seasons.

When I met my first god-person, they were
a frustrated blood, a look in—

Once, I washed the feet
of an elder woman
in front of the entire congregation. I turned my head left,

as if waiting for my sin to leave.
I have become a casualty, a reincarnation of death-practice,

not unlike Christ,
with his Sisyphus wrist, and his want of dusk.

My grandmother has turned looking into a language, a season
whittled down to degrees.

The almost Mary-voiced
creature. This helix-figured woman. Her right hand
is dark purple,

thick-skinned as muscadine.
                    I rub her hand, her hair.
Her hand rises, a limb I bend into the shade.

Her new voice is always a surprise and
always not.

Death/Machine/Ruin

~~One. 1969.~~ *~~William O'Neal.~~* ~~Sir,~~ I have ~~never lost function or focus. I did my job and remained silent. Fred was a friend, but now dead and can't do anymore harm.~~ A good ~~man, but witnessing a room so close to death has taught me that even "good" can be a tattered arm holding back progress. He was~~ a good ~~man, yes, but he was no~~ King. ~~He soldiered black men, exchanging feardom for freedom. Sir, I hope this was enough to prove~~ myself. ~~I hope this was enough to wash away my theft and papers. Because this is all I wanted to be. To~~ be black with dignity.

~~Two. 1990.~~ *~~William O'Neal.~~* ~~Uncle, last week, a man ran in front of moving traffic on Westbound Lanes of the Eisenhower~~ Expressway. ~~I haven't seen him since. He was a neighbor.~~ A soft-~~spoken, silent of a man. He must have been looking for a reply to return to him like~~ color ~~that leapt from a pale face. Soon it will be King Day, where black bodies will crowd on the road~~ like ~~wet sand. I am lost in the history of~~ money. ~~I mean currency. A compromise without debt.~~

Grace Division

I like repeating myself. That turn
of the glass to find your print.

       It is like being called to
in the same exact way, every Sunday.

During my second stay at Cypress Creek Hospital,
I held my little maroon journal
as ammunition.

Reclaiming yourself is a skill

like warring is a skill. The hull and mull
of the white space

in my stomach held a religious
ache. I didn't sleep for days.

       The meds
were a beating metronome, a metamorphic
season. To reclaim myself, I promised this sinning
would save me.

I am war again.

Tried talking to a knife half-wanting
the husk to outgrow me. I won't leave

things out. I would dream often
of turning a knife

into my brother, but he would carry on living
in my dreaming.

I only let N visit me.

He was always stronger than me.
On a drunken night, N taught me how to knife-fight

with a spoon in his living room.
My grandfather would carry with him
a razor in his boot

the size of his foot. I pocketed N's pistol
on the way to his brother's house, and

I ended up hiding it in the back of his green truck

leaving the door unlocked. We drank so much of death
we passed the bread without crumbling.

    But those mistakes are not gods—

but shards upswept from the concrete.
The broken think division will add to themselves,

        the risk in the mining of diamonds.
The weight of his pistol
pulled me down like children begging. Finding family

in a psych ward
is like abuse feeding wounds,

like switching places to better bear witness.
  The turning ends where it begins.

Two men turning god over like an apple
in their hands. A cold yolk

teasing breaking. A sharp mirror warring itself
into a witness.

To those who count suicide as a spiritual warfare addendum

Souls lull
to lust.
Slots us
out, louts.
Lost us—
O us, out
to lots. Too
lost.
Lust
tolls us
to soot lots,
to stulls. O
slut souls—
Us too!
Tut! Lotus—
Lo!
So to
lust.
Us lost solus
sots.

Royal

GOD IS MY GOLDEN AGAINST WICKED MINDED BOY & MEN LIKE—
ROLAND DID—ME OF MEN LIKE—DANIEL—DID ME I PUT FOOL OUT
NOW THERE MORE AROUND IN TRAILER HOMES GOD TELL I GOT
FIND AWAY TO LEAVE WORRISOMES—INDIANS AND WORRISOME
NIGGERS BOYS BEFORE I KILL BOY & MEN LIEN AND ATTACH THE
LOT IS BASTARD'S EVIL EYED KILLERS

IN THE VOICE OF ROYAL ROBERTSON FOR ROYAL ROBERTSON

ALL MORNIN' I WILL BREAK MY TEETH INTO
WORDS MY PAINTINGS—HANG HUSHED LIKE
HARLOTS IN MY HOUSE HEAT-HEAVY THROUGH THE WINDOW
IN BALDWIN LOUISIANA EACH WINDOW—AN EYE
FOLLOWIN' ME NOT CLOSING UNTIL THE—SUN
DIES—HAUL US ALL THERE ARE HOLES IN A PERSON
A SUN WILL FILL OR BIBLICAL WIND—ROYAL VERSE 5:97—
BEHIND OUR HOLES WE ARE SMALL YOKES TRYING TO SEE
THE OTHER DAY A SMALL MAN CAME TO MY DOOR
HE SAID "PROPHET, THE WHORE DOESN'T TELL YOUR
BASTARD CHILDREN ABOUT YOU NO MORE"
THE SMALL MAN STANDS PLASTERED AT THE DOOR
ODD-COLORED EYES AND SKIN MY FRAMES HANG
LIKE HOOKERS IN MY FRONT YARD IT TAKES HEAT
TO HURT THEM—I AM THE PROPHET—WHO PROVES POWER
IN HANDS SOMETIMES WHEN THE LITTLE MEN VISIT—GOD
THE DRIVER—THEY SPEAK IN FOREIGN SPITS
AND THE SPACESHIP NEVER SPEAKS
CAN I KEEP LIGHT BEHIND MY TEETH? A WORD
BREAKS ME ALL MORNIN'—*PUNISHMENT*—
THE VOWELS FILL AND HIT LIKE SPIT—*PUNISHMENT*—

LITTLE MAN! I TOLD YOU TO PICK ME UP YESTERDAY
THE MANHATTANS LEFT TOO IN YOUR TRUCK WITH
YOUR CHILDREN—MY ONCE LOVELY ADELL SLEPT LIKE
JEZEBEL IN FIRE THE BURNIN' LIAR BURNIN' MOTHER!
SLANDER—NO—SAY *TRY* SEVEN TIMES OVER AND I
WILL SEAR THE WORDS FROM YOUR MOUTH WITH MY GRIEF TEETH
I CURSE THE WINDOWS AND IT CLOSES ON ME LIKE A FIST
I TRUST THE WALLS I HEAR—ON THE WALLS I HANG
PAINTINGS AND PICTURES LIKE PROPHESIES HERE
LIKE WHORES IN THIS HOUSE WHERE I CAN HOLD THEM

Man in a Hole

When last was it when

you couldn't distinguish blackness from a hole

in the earth?—

I can see now too! How the creased

shadow mimics my standing here.

The hole that holds Linda, too,

is black, and the handholes

that held her before this one

were black as well.

At the base of this stone, the vase hands

let the bouquet rest on its neck. Its neck-scent reddening.

Red has the tendency

to stand out in any assortment of colors, its accent

shadowing the brights.

If we could rely on the body's timing,

we could make a color mean resilience

or surety,

or I could've loved her or married her

alive—

—if at least for protection, to separate her

from that death-rhythm we call *pass over silence*.

I carry with me a Houston crease in my brain.

It helps me forget that life once was a metaphor

for afterlife.

Over there,

even the trees are scared

asking forgiveness, their bodies wanting to be seen

as the night puts on its black mask.

And it takes a whole lot of time for me

to come back to this mass garden

and lapse back

to remember the man who removed her life

black hands look like mine.

    I couldn't look her mother

in the eye. At the wake, I kept getting second glances

from her cousins. I wanted to tell them, I am not of mask,

but of a dark mass mattering

in public spaces—and I wanted to tell them nothing of it.

    I'd wrestle with my face,

but there are limits to this. A madness

in which I am a soft cloak letting drop.

How could I not be born in the new birth in the aftermath of this?—

I've been saying sorry all the way into the future,

where all my memory is scared for the hereafter.

In a Houston crease in the earth,

over there, with cranes and cement, the city sirens itself

in a cistern.

I pass over her, half-shadowing her yard home.

I am a time-sensitive thing.

I hold my hole-mask accountable.

De███/█a████/R███

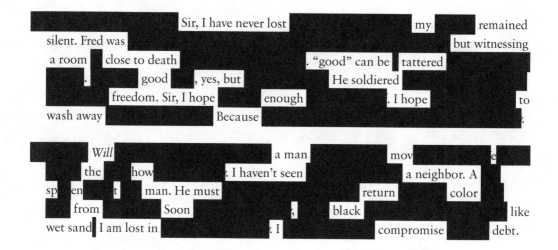

           Sir, I have never lost   my   remained
silent. Fred was   but witnessing
a room   close to death   . "good" can be   tattered
     .   good   , yes, but   He soldiered
      freedom. Sir, I hope   enough   . I hope   to
wash away   Because   .

       Will   a man   mov   e
   the   how   . I haven't seen   a neighbor. A
sp en   t   man. He must   return   color
  from   Soon   ,   black   like
wet sand I am lost in   . I   compromise   debt.

Elegy for Threats with Grace

I sit with a word like *schizophrenic* until it becomes a color.

I spent so many years being afraid to be black, that now
    I am only afraid of silence,

        or the silence that it brings.

A hunch that what is born in the earth
will tear through it.

The thread of history. The threat of history.

What's dredged up from earth is sturdy as teeth.

When I speak quietly, I am speaking to a family
in Estill Springs, Tennessee

or Spring, Texas
saying, *I am sorry*.

Like how God was sorry when he witnessed
the way Skirrid Mountain split

in two like Christ's wrists crucified.

In every old black man I come across
I see my grandfather.

His blue overalls hanging off his body
like his youngest child

who was named after him and who died
of AIDS or overdose.

His name was Henry, though he went by Clay—

Some nights, I feel as crazy as I did that night,

screaming through the streets,
swinging a knife at bushes and mailboxes.

Jim McIlherron shot the two white men dead
when they harassed him.

The rocks they threw at him
were like unnamed pockets of earth.

It took only a few days for the mob to find him
with torches the color of rust, and chained

him to a hickory tree, setting his body afire,
a light they took in with slurs and fists.

As a child in school, I would go so long
without speaking that people thought I was
a mute.

A child with words only inside him
like a hidden family is inside.

But now, on these days I don't know what to do
with my hands.

Language is like a month ending
with a fire.

Royal Robertson lost his mind in the South too.
And died in Houston.

He was a sign painter who painted little men
with big eyes. They'd speak to him of raptures
and spaceships.

But he let them too far in—

R., you are not a prophet and
I don't believe in God anymore.

My hands are threats,
songs long enough to become prayers.

J., there were bars of hot iron against your skin,
leaving a valley glow.

You didn't wince or cringe.

You cursed those who burned you.
Never losing your nerve. Not breaking
until your last breath.

I admire and despise that kind of perseverance.
    Yet I don't speak of it.

Like how much my indecision is decision.

t /   a   /R

One   never
                    can't   harm A g od
          to death   a   n   d   back
    . He was   t he   soldier
              I hope   i was   . I hope   to
          theft   this   black   dignity.

              Un   man
                                                        a
soft   man.   reply to   him
              .   it will   crowd   the road
    wet   . I am   money. I   promise   out   .

Bayou City Season

Saying *grace* is a matter of suffering.
    I think of the rain as heaven
surrendering.
    I earned this comedown.

When we are dislocated, the hues
    of our faces change, greening
like the eye of an infant—

In the South, we have an affinity
    for water.
As though, to re-earth
    ourselves we must first remove
our shoes.

No one dead has no place
    to go.
When they are black,
    they can make myths
out of any large body

of water. Everyone who I love in Houston
    is a terrible fish
swallowing the air from my Texas body.

All that September, all I wanted to be
      was a southern thing
again.
      But remained

in the east like a citrine
      stone. After swallowing
the word X,
      I paced

my room for several days.
      Language would have you believe
that several means seven.

There is always an agitation in lyric.
      The way our names match
our faces is too linear

for myth. In the West Indies,
      they used to name hurricanes
      after saints.
As if naming you we could control you.

Harvey, I must assume,
      is the name of a man
speechified on the second story
      of his bare-floored apartment—

For seven days, I considered praying to him,
      and the X opened up
wide inside me as a new
      language scar.

I hoped to trade myself for Houston—
      biting the inside of my cheek.

Every year you are like this.
    Riding this injury
like a bison embarrassed

by its own brutality complex.
    The city, he himself, cannot sin.

All this new rhythm has left you
    and you have done nothing wrong.

Every southern storm is baptismic.
    The way we relearn to rehearse
thirst like an activist.

But I tell you, there are even
    some sane saints who refuse
water during a fast.

Grace & Separation

There's a photo of Laura Nelson, a rope between her and a tree.
The backdrop, more trees.

A person in the picture is bound to history.

Bound to the same color.

And there's a sculpture of Mary Turner in bronze
holding her stomach.

She is childless.

Her husband, Hazel, died a day before her
but with less spectacle.

I always thought my mother was crazy for the way she wore blackness
like a new wristwatch.

And with her skin beige and hazel,
I thought she must have been compensating for something.

Grief is a healthy disease
unlike forgetting.

The body has more than one soul.
The main soul is behind the forehead
and the second soul is in the pupils.

There's the world of the photograph vs. the imagined world.

In a picture everything is placed like a target.

I always believed my mother was crazy for not wanting to kill herself
on days when her body

would no longer do what she needed it to

like love, make love, or speak—

At noon on Sunday in 1918, the mob found Mary
8 months pregnant and took her near Folsom Bridge, over the Little River,
and tied her by her ankles.

Her sin was speaking.
We are difficult in the sense that we can't un-God ourselves.

In the photos of my grandmother, she's always small
and scowling like a cub.

When she was young,
she would never leave home without a blade in her wig.
Outside of a club, a man wanted to fight her.

She pulled the blade from her wig
and cut his chest like tree bark.
The next morning, she went to the police station crying,

saying that she might have killed a man.
They laughed at her.

God tries out different combinations of mothers with children,
rearranging them at the first sign of uncleanliness.

The white men broke Mary's stomach in two with a knife.
What was cut from her was something more than human.

The two cries they let out didn't reach where the two colors met.
The brown body meeting the brown dirt.
Earth's natural law of what America births.

My mother was never crazy, only quiet—
A girl grown woman.

In a photo in 1981, she looked like two cries, a batch of berries
held close enough together not to burst.

Its insides having dark-blue ink like skin.

A Consequence (Passing)

my sin's wisdom evolves slow | as so regressive | knife-heavy in the back |

in the back | seat where I am part seen | and half-reflected |

the knife is misplaced | falling | out |

of my pocket as an accidental rhyme |

i hate when I am like this in June |

it is a month like September, a self | induced |

fever | where I swear it's seasonal |

my reflection is doing the double-work | with outpatient patience |

i wasn't hurt. I wasn't |

wronged | I clenched onto | as with a river-stone jaw |

in my furthest self of my shame |

i am black in back |

of a police car in 2011's June |

blacked | out and banging my head against the car |

window and hysterical |

crying that I do not want to go to jail and be raped |

because my mother | was raped |

in Christian speak |

i was told over | again | throughout my life |

that I am watched |

by God | a scarcity | in which I am |

the last kind of | this silence |

as my ten-year-old self, I would sneak-listen |

to Em's album | mouthing along to his | horrorcore |

of murdering | gay men | and women |

and I failed | them | tact | lessly |

i ask forgiveness | as if asking for seconds | in the late |

evening | my self-laws |

are a cheap hanging desert moon | and I hate to bother you |

elsewhere in the appetite still | an adolescent |

in the throes of a fight | with my brother |

i would call him a *faggot* | because |

i could think of no word more hurt |

held and etching |

now the word bleeds |

me as much as *nigger* |

| (bleeds lunacy bruising me) |

i recommend you sit by yourself |

and face away from |

the sun. You are waiting for |

the *loveafter* | aren't you |

the soft streak |

that shrieks through your skin |

like Jesus's nigga crown |

your skin is the last habit |

you must not break |

the | *thereafter* and the |

therebefore |

Ten Stories

The length of my mother's hair stopped growing.

There's a picture of four women in pink I keep in my wallet. I left it out in the sun.

Now little red ovals have appeared like snow on them.

Last week, during an accidental sleep I dreamt of stabbing my brother again.

And the knife was bold and broke like a bone.

Ozara told her cousin Kayla she loved her while she was sleeping.
Then my mother looked at her with a look that minussed time.

Last year, when N tried to shoot himself in front of me, I fought the gun away from him for a
full minute.
In that moment,
we were grappling *forever* in our hands.

Driving home from Ratan's wedding, I knew death was a ripped piece of paper.

After I told Ozara I would be leaving, a crisis opened up inside of her like a red trap door.

Death waited half a day to tell me what it did to Linda. I drove between two hours to reach them.

That morning me and my mother thought my sister was murdered, we noticed how black we both were. How full of static.

My grandmother would always say, "Blessed coming in, blessed

going out,"

so I was told.

WE

The Mirror Myth

in regard to my mother

See,

this is how the lyric will tear

you in two.

My mother's lord

mimics the love sound makes.

I mimicked her head-down quiet speak

way of living.

I swear

it is a rattled thing.

To some.

Yet to me

it carries some tear-wet feet

to a city-like citadel on tall stulls

where we all slip into survival.

And as black as that is, it is closer to her earth.

Some nights, I believe in God again

just to turn my disdain toward him

for taking ownership for her strength.

And I don't know much for strength.

Since a boy, I've been practicing her, her

ways of speaking and of not.

In its air they both can sound

like little blanks, false starts.

Here,

in the myth I prayed for her,

there is no violence in silence.

When I began school, my skin began to darken away

from hers.

Less like honey

my beige bruised

like a wound pulled in every direction.

Word choice is cruel in sovereignty.

So when I say

my mother would use her spit

to clean my eyes

before the school bus,

I mean her Jesus hands

look like a dove cowering.

I say all this to say God

is in my mother's hair.

And as so, this twinning never hurts.

When she blurs, I blur.

Two too-close-proximity similes—

Quietness is not the same

as practice.

When she was at the age I was

when I first learned how to write,

she had already been raped

and her hair was still

red.

I rarely bled and never

broke a bone.

My mother's head-down face

would read her blue Bible

to herself by her nightstand.

Speech does only half

of what eyes can do.

Our voices crack when love

comes up short,

Is this it of the grace you set?

Even when I'd hear I got God

about me

I knew I was just practicing.

As if my body never was

what it was.

As if the Lord troubles you

in two

for your womb to wound blue

so he is needed

like a midwife asking permission.

To those who think I won't set this country afire with me still in it

To try, poets prey. Treetop to root. Pots poorer. Peers too proper. Too white. Pretty pets, prep

petty toys; pottery. Peyote pots, props to rot. O prototype or property. Yet preps proper toys.

Troops retort, poets retry—O tore ropes to ropery, treeports. Try perters too—*To poets' report*.

A Constant Conjunction

1

Let the body speak for itself on Sundays. How dark the low-hanging fruit looked
from an angle, where I stood at the altar waiting for my speech to become
rhythmic. There's an awful epistemology behind how I can't forget the faces of the
black women at Northchase Church. They loved me like a lioness loves her leaves.
Comforted sleep.

Curse me.

I can't compare to where I stand now to where I barely stood at the bedfoot of a righteous life to
help remove her shoes. But still, in front of the congregation, we removed their shoes—us three
teens on our knees in front of three older black women near a white bowl and white wet towel,
dahlias fragranced in the water. We cleaned their feet, tiny saints; we were below like below a
cross.

Church Joshua was part of this cycle, precursor to melancholia, young pastor like Baldwin,
mimicking his pantomime shapes. I wore the awful repetition like an American smile. The hard
work of the believer. A short service rifled between two long spirituals. A family of black-
blistered Christians taking in whiteness like addicts.

Curse me 'til I'm dead, church me ███████████████████
███████████████ slave in my head.

With my same Christ-voice once used for reminiscing scriptures, I will report poetry with.

2

Grace does not belong to you. All signifiers reverberate—as to re-verb a thing.

Runful.

Church me.

From gospel to blues like breaking into derangement.

I mostly think diction is about timing. And words carry the dead like henchmen.

And we'd wait for the choir's siren like a fool cutting his tongue to accent his speech—

█████████████ dead ████████████████████████
Th███████e████████other slave in m████e█████

In the myth where Jesus accidently cuts his hair, he plants its patch in the dirt waiting for an oceanic spur.

Grace moves like this.

The soft relays.

A new arithmetic.

A holy holder.

Jesus, I will not give you my hair or my eyes.

Boy Joshua would mock Bartimaeus in the 1979 Jesus film, proclaiming, "I can see, I can see."

Now Joshua cries at the Syracuse Hancock International Airport, listening to Frank Ocean.

I learned to be holy without holiness, to be black without God's willingness to get me back.

Forgive Joshua Forgive Joshua Forgive Joshua Forgive Joshua Forgive Joshua Forgive Joshua
Forgive Joshua Forgive Joshua Forgive Joshua Forgive Joshua
Forgive Joshua Forgive Joshua
Forgive Joshua Forgive Joshua Forgive Joshua Forgive Joshua
Forgive Joshua Forgive Joshua
Forgive Joshua Forgive Joshua Forgive Joshua Forgive Joshua
Forgive Joshua Forgive Joshua
Forgive Joshua Forgive Joshua Forgive Joshua Forgive Joshua
Forgive Joshua Forgive Joshua
Forgive Joshua   Joshua   Joshua   Joshua
        Joshua   Joshua
                Joshua Forgive Joshua
        Joshua Forgive Joshua
Forgive   Forgive   Forgive   Forgive Joshua
Forgive Yehoshua
Forgive Joshua Forgive Joshua Forgive Yehoshua Forgive Joshua
Forgive Ye   s
Forgive   u Forgive   Forgive Yeshua Forgive Yeshua
Forgive Yeshua Forgive Yesh
Forgive Yeshua Forgive Yeshua Forgive Yeshua Forgive Yeshua
Forgive Yeshua Forgive Yeshua Forgive Joshua Forgive Yes
                Forgive Yeshua Forgive Joshua Forgi   Yeshua
Forgive Joshua Forgive Yeshua Forgive Joshua Forgive Yeshua
Forgive Joshua Forgiv Yeshua Forgive Jesus Forgive Yeshua
Forgive Yeshua Forgive Joshua Forgive Jesus Forgive Yeshua
Forgive Jesus Forgive Jesus Forgive Jesus Forgive Joshua Forgive
Joshua Forgive Yeshua Forgive Yeshua Forgive Yeshua Forgive
Yeshua Forgive Yeshua Forgive Yeshua Forgive Yeshua Forgive
Yeshua Forgive Yeshua Forgive Yeshua Forgive Yeshua Forgive
Yeshua Forgive Yeshua Forgive Yeshua Forgive Yeshua Forgive
Yeshua Forgive Yeshua Forgive Yeshua Forgive Yeshua Forgive
Yeshua Forgive Yeshua Forgive Yeshua Forgive Yeshua Forgive
Yeshua Forgive Yeshua Forgive Yeshua Forgive Yeshua Forgive
Yeshua Forgive Yeshua Forgive Yeshua Forgive Yeshua Forgive
Yeshua Forgive Yeshua Forgive Yeshua Forgive Yeshua Forgive
Yeshua Forgive Yeshua Forgive Yeshua Forgive Yeshua Forgive
Yeshua Forgive Yeshua Forgive Yeshua Forgive Yeshua Forgive

Yeshua Forgive Yeshua Forgive Yeshua Forgive Yeshua Forgive
Yeshua For

Forgive Joshua Forgive Jesus Forgive   Forgive
Forgive   Forgive

                              give Joshua   a
     give

          Joshua Forgive Yeshua Forgive Yeshua Forgive Yeshua
Forgive Yeshua Forgive Yeshua Forgive Yeshua Forgive Yeshua
Forgive Yeshua Forgive Yeshua Forgive Yeshua Forgive Yeshua
Forgive Yeshua Forgive Yeshua Forgive Yeshua Forgive Yeshua
Forgive Yeshua Forgive Yeshua Forgive Yeshua Forgive Yeshua
Forgive Yeshua Forgive Yeshua Forgive Yeshua Forgive Yeshua
Forgive Yeshua Forgive Yeshua Forgive Yeshua Forgive Yeshua
Forgive Yeshua Forgive Yeshua Forg   For   us
          a   Jesus

                         Forgive Jesus Forgive Jesus
Forgive Jesus Forgive Jesu Forgive Jesus Forgive Jesus Forgive
Jesus Forgive Jesus Forgive Jesus Forgive Jesus Forgive Jesus
Forgive Jesus Forgive Jesus Forgive Jesus Forgive Joshua Forgive
Jesus Forgive Jesus
Forgive Jesus Forgive Jesus Forgive Jesus Forgive Jesus Forgive
Jesus Forgive Jesus Forgive Joshua Forgive Jesus Forgive Jesus
Forgive Royal Forgive Jesus Sweet Royal Forgive Royal

Giving Jim Grace

for Jim McIlherron

Lyric is a lie to the sentence and snow is a silent engine.
While in it, all I can imagine is a slow torch prodigal

in its returning. I entered your story, Jim, like a crow to a cloud.
Leaving Houston, all I could see was the potential of snow

on my fingers. And I know that I notice blackness
when separated from blackness. And know that I am a motor
running off of grief. Jim, a hundred years before me,

you carried your pistol shiny as a broken mirror.
And after reading what happened to you, I knelt down
by my bedside like looking for lost change.

The pathetic way I left my family in Houston was the pathetic way
I found you, as if family was something less visible in the night.
As if the snow somehow makes the night less of itself.

The only language I choose to acknowledge is distance. No,
I was away from all I was meant to know, an animal unaware
that its stripes were scars. Telling the truth could kill us.

I reach for stories in dead black men for catharsis. In the driveway,
I unpeel the frost—as a gauze. There are truths I've never told relatives,

like how others' memories can speak to you like good rain.
Shall I call you brother or uncle then? *Jesus Christ!*—

Like a lie I whir into irony—how only kin can sentence
the sentence. Jim, your white light still lights and breathes in cursive.

On my skin where I picked at quills, I wrote:
Grief is a happiness too. Suddenly, feeling family

as opposed to knowing family, we can bear these truths.
I was heavy about myself because snow does something
to you the way flesh burns memory into you—

And I know if lyric lies to us, it must still reveal
a skin perfected in its low glow.

Prophet Royal Robertson

In the voice of Adell Robertson for Adell Robertson

After a night of night-

fishing we take the small catfish home to feed

the babies.   We cut

off its head with its still flashing mud-faced grin.

After the babies are done, we exchange looks of

   you next, you next.

What we saw was what we thought.

Looking we *STILL* in the moment

      of waiting

and I do not know this word.

Sweet Royal, you wear the *ELSEWHERE* like paint,

like mud under your nails.

But our most worked signifier is not in the hands

speaking from the *KNOW THIS WORD*.

Giving Mary Grace

for Mary Turner

History will submit to you | I will too |

Eventually when we are color-pleased | when your dirt speaks |

I will be left | dumb-still |

I won't refer you back to life |

There's been enough of that |

I falter | in guilt | at your reanimating |

Now I am trying to unbeast you |

Having walked with myth and imagination |

I thought I counted every stone. The walls |

grew closer |

| I walk in a terrible circle |

Should I quiet my poet, yes |

I wanted to die too, yes |

But concealed that adolescence | like a hymn |

through me |

Through me wasn't always the answer |

| I am black people |

and am a series of decisions |

Shall I let my *again* speak for me, no |

Agains stain the clear water |

Can I offer you up to speak, if |

Only if | you are compelled to |

I wasn't finished with myself, I |

Where story and desire | collide |

with terrible friction |

How full of stories are you, many |

I wake up late too often |

how I am   inside of night |

as in, is your strength blacker than my weakness |

is black? |

       |

     |

        |

To those who know how to unthreat oneself

In staying alive, my decision is my indecision.

The Worst Houston

for Linda

When the body is unbodied, all that is left are myths.
A seasonal city failing to know itself.

A celestial break in the air.
As a child, when I'd break my toy, I'd hide it.

When I finally lose my mind, my feet
will be the first to go. Sunday mornings,

David would call, asking me to visit the grave with him,
and he's on his way.

I live with the fear
of all the women in my life dying before me.

When he arrives, we get on our knees
to clean the granite.

From afar, I bet the body
looks like a black dog

behind water. This death is Houston

at its very worst. More worse even
than at the death of Carl Hampton, that Panther who curved
like a branch at his end.

Back then, my father was a boy watching
the Panthers march along Allen Parkway Village.

When I was a boy of five, my hand touched
the hot kitchen iron with the curiosity of my five-year-old mouth
kissing my neighbor.

At the wake, in a Catholic ritual that I did not understand,
David wrapped a white cloth around my head for you.

Later Sundays at the grave,
I'd think, *We deserve beauty here too.*

We clean your stone, a stained-glass plate, your small
oval photo, looking up.

Like you, sometimes, I want to open

up the sky, climb inside like a sunroof
to a blue sports car.

I, too, only love God when I'm greedy.

When I am home from the grave,
walking into my mother's room is like walking into a coma.

She wants me to wash my feet
and doesn't want me touching her.

On those Sundays, I'd usually arrive at the grave
a little early, minutes before David

thinking maybe it is too much to talk to you,
but I talk to you

saying things like:

Help me find another word for sympathy.

Or

sorry.

And wanting you to say:

Come to my home,
touch my hands.

I'll keep whatever you leave.

Grace Engine

I love all the dead,
both at the moment they unwed

themselves of shame
and before that.

The two men who think they will never die
are two opposing laws:

the will to live and the will to live a little longer.

In a room, in June, full of bike parts, empty Bic lighters and grease,
N takes ten minutes to open the door

and I am afraid for him.

We are like brothers, like canyons, a fulmination
between us, all red,
all black.

My real brother once while half-asleep put a hot iron against his cheek
thinking it was the phone.

It is hard to tell the truth.
And it is hard to be in a room with so many words,
the walls with holes the size of fists.

N pulled the pistol from his jeans
and placed it in the space between his ear and eye
like creating an extra sense

and pointing to it.

Once before, he told me if I were to suicide
he would piss on my grave.

"Again" says: *There will be a god at the end of me.*

Assata Shakur says: *Some people spell god with one "o"*
while others spell it with two.

To be in a room like this
full of white ghosts and ropes tied

together in little black knots
is the opposite of being anywhere.

After I fought the gun away from him, that hinge
of metal between my fingers was human-animal.

Our fingers in the holes in the metal
made us whole as a woman

before machining out her second life.

Giving Laura Grace

for Laura Nelson and her son, L. D. Nelson

Like the time I mistook a bridge for a tree, I am
    waiting for the poem to correct
me. Where afraid and ashamed
    sister-touch.

And all the swear-blood in me brews
    in the fist of my stomach.

I wrote to you once before,
    Laura,
and failed.

    So I won't write about your lynched body anymore.
You are not my mother, so I have no moral
    contract with you.

If I did, I'd probably still
    only have stories for you.

Like in kindergarten when I punched a black
    boy in the chest.
He punched me too,

    and we cried together
as if this was our shared code for confession.

Or the story where
I was in the midst of a dirt-fight with a black boy
   my size in a large open square

where a house would soon be built.
   Our hands threw the sand through the air—
moving like a clapper in a bell. Where some
   ended up in my throat,

with that little piece of earth lost
   in my mouth staining my voice and what
came out next. And my mother took a hot face-
   towel to my tongue.

I'm sorry, but I think hurting something black
   became a habit. When I say *earth*, I mean God.

Maybe it was a living root bridge
   is what I'd tell myself.
And maybe, black people are born with cedar seeds
   in us.

I used to only believe in death by
   habit. Yet the sound
of a woman screaming still frightens me.

   Though I promise not to martyr you or mother you,
I promise the same for L. D. too.

   Next year, when I am older
and know better,
   I will visit Okemah, Oklahoma,

and dig.
    And I will plant my hands in the soil
and slide my blood back into my wrist like a stubborn vein
      and wait for your nothing.

Grace as Kin as Sin as Skin

it's as if since
birth   i've
been   hearing
tar   with   the
hard   *R*   you
ready   for   the
synesthesia
of   inner   anti
blackness
that   kept   you
from   looking
others   in   the
eye   too   only
look   for   good
when   i'm
greedy   for   all
that   is   holy   is
closed   the
body   never
was   what   it
was   self
hatred   a   gift
the   mystic
mistook   to   be
mastered   all
art   in   the
sense   of
giving
oneself   to   be
in   this   "we"
nod in god in love
nod to our kin folk
music is my nigga
in me turns to
God runs to the
river   when
his   thirst   is
birth

grace   as
june   as
change   as
burden   as
sin   as
separation
as
september
as   heights
as   land   as
snow   as
return   as
horn   as   self
as
apparition
as   kin   as
heat   as
houston   as
rooms   as
~~death~~   as
song   as   skin
as ours

i   am   called
by   poetry   to
my   name   in
music   like
yehoshua
you   are   god
too   but   too
many   others
are   too   i   was
tying
blackness   to
blackness
back   when   i
held   my
niggadom   in
myself   like   a
river
thirsting   a
body   never
closing   in
that   holy   run
run

67

A Confession

for my grandfather Henry Pearl Stewart

the poem is better than me   it breaks me where all my flesh lies
something black in me broke   felt like a crypt curse   unbellying
light-seeds from my genetic memory   i speak to my grandfather
in the language of a breakdown

    Henry Pearl Stewart—a man so stubborn he would pull out his loose teeth
    with pliers   like ruined potatoes   rather than going to the dentist
    they'd call him Pistol P.   as though his magnum would accent his paragon

i've never been to Alabama   except to go through it   the mapped South
stretches like a threshold   going in and out   an ouroboros
of heat-light   in the cesarian-cruel land shrapnel is unearthed   let's go of our *let go's*

    i'd like to think all the dead are reasonable   was his fear of snakes
    unreasonable   near his fear of being hung?—

Mattie Jones sings to the skull of Bull Connor   beneath Bermudagrass

    and before I'll be a slave, i'll be buried in my grave
    the best way to expose grace is through singing   and there's a song
    in the curse   in the trees following us.

Pearl's lynched siblings   his sister   was drowned in Birmingham
his brother   learned death   from walking on the same side of the sidewalk
where a white woman was   in Birmingham
i heard there were more   but i don't know the siblings' names   yet

except Pearl said he left Birmingham because a woman   put a Hoodoo curse
on him and not this   because death   can be a many-eyed   problem
solving bargain.

as i try   not to carry names   as weapons   or myth them into meaning
i must still learn   myself alive   trauma, like the poem   must look both ways
to look at itself

    what can stretch from the dead to   living as an unbroken line break?—
    and what else can you learn about affinity   today?—

i love my grandfather's hands   he held a figure 8 over our heads
like two Christ-crowns—shame

    on you, Joshua, for blowing yourself out of proportion   like this
    with your six-breakdown self   you are no single thing—shame
    let loose like a lynch in me

though i cannot live up to the expectation of black strength   in blackness   here i am
and thinking of this black insanity—   uplifted from the root

    i must be forgiven somewhere   for thinking blackness was the curse

i tied myself to Pearl   a thin rope that snapped   a branch bullied into submission
or like an 8   snaps   again   again—

As I Grace Myself into a Rephrasing Freedom

Us

In the last dream I had of my grandfather he let me touch his hands like Jesus
with something to prove. He might've been in the opposite of *place*. I say,
"I am sorry," like the trees are sorry. Grew god

from their tongues as in to better know the wind's brutal trial. The leaves like hair,
barren. Pointed their stalk fingers as to heaven. God must be black for us to peddle
in time backwards. Mary Turner might've said, "You motherfuckers are wrong"
to the men who lynched her husband.

When I choose to fill my hands with *stay here*, I know the soul can't bear being
in the stomach any longer. It moves like a sprain to our feet.

Us too

I've been meaning to tell you why I've always loved myself. In the first dream
I'll have after waking from running from myself my insides will stretch in every direction
like a machining vein.

Each line as an unbent bar funneling blood and what's beneath blood. I'll say,
"I won't turn back time, nor be stripped from Negritude," but hold a photo empty
as a church, shaking off its ghost-speak—white then not, and reach for that minor
god. I am *repetition*.

That frame like a sin, like an ex-slave planting redwood trees,
like how the wind from a mouth can coax the flame into living.

Notes

William O'Neal was an FBI informant who infiltrated the Chicago sector of the Black Panther Party as a bodyguard whose information and participation led to the murder of Fred Hampton and Mark Clark by the police on December 6, 1969. In 1990, William O'Neal committed suicide. It was suspected by his uncle that William's guilt for what he had done to Hampton led to his suicide. "Death/Machine/Ruin," "D███/█a██/R██," and " t / a /R " are all written in the voice of William O'Neal, revealing more/less in each erasure. In "Death/Machine/Ruin," part one is written to FBI agent Roy Mitchell, who William worked with as an informant, and part two is written to William's uncle, who was the last person to see him alive.

Royal Robertson lived in Baldwin, Louisiana, for most of his life. He married Adell Brent in 1955 and they had twelve children together. Royal was a sign painter. He suffered from schizophrenia, and his hallucinations and paranoias made him think that his wife was cheating on him and that he wasn't the father of their children. Adell ended up leaving him and taking all their children with her. She became a minister. Royal stayed in Louisiana and built up a great disdain for his ex-wife and all women in general. He immersed himself into his artwork. Now being a complete recluse, he created worlds of his own through his art. He referred to himself as "Prophet Royal Robertson" and had numerous visions, believing he was visited by aliens and spaceships driven by God. Some hallucinations had aliens depicting the "End of Day" and warning him that his wife's adultery may have led to a worldwide women conspiracy against him. He surrounded his house inside and out with paintings of his visions, which alienated him from his neighbors. He also used biblical prophecies and science fiction in his work. He died from a heart attack in 1997 at the age of sixty. The poem "Royal" is a ballad written in the voice of Royal Robertson and the poem "Prophet Royal Robertson" is written in the voice of Adell.

Jim McIlherron was an African American man from Tennessee who was lynched by a mob in 1918. He was lynched for defending himself, shooting and killing two of the three white men who were harassing him by throwing rocks at him. He is referenced in the poem "Elegy for Threats with Grace," and the poem "Giving Jim Grace" is addressed to him.

In 2017, Hurricane Harvey made landfall in Texas, devastating the city of Houston along with many other cities. The poem "Bayou City Season" is about the hurricane.

Laura Nelson was an African American woman from Oklahoma who was raped and lynched by a mob in 1911 alongside her fourteen-year-old son, L. D Nelson. They were both charged with the murder of a deputy sheriff. There is a well-known photo of the lynching. This photo is referenced in the poem "Grace & Separation," and the poem "Giving Laura Grace" is addressed to Laura and L. D. Nelson.

Mary Turner was an African American woman from Georgia who was lynched by a mob in 1918. She was lynched for speaking out against the lynching of her husband, Hazel "Hayes" Turner. She is referenced in the poems "Grace & Separation" and "As I Grace Myself into a Rephrasing Freedom," and the poem "Giving Mary Grace" is addressed to her.

In the poem "A Constant Conjunction," there's an erasure from Kendrick Lamar's song "The Blacker the Berry."

In the poem "Grace Engine," there's a quote by Assata Shakur taken from her open letter to Pope John Paul II in 1998.

Acknowledgments

A huge thank you to the publications that gave these poems a chance and took them in. These poems and earlier versions of them have appeared in the following journals:

Black Warrior Review, *Cobra Milk*, *Conduit Magazine*, *Grist Journal*, *Group Head Magazine*, *Indiana Review*, *Public Poetry Magazine*, *The Rumpus*, *Southeast Review*, *Sybil Journal*, and *TriQuarterly*.

The creation of this book could not have been seen through without the support of countless people and organizations. Thank you to my cohort, professors, and friends at Syracuse University. A special thanks to Vt, Ross, Bridget, Zeynep, Ariel, Nghiem, Anthony, Salome, and Isabel. And thank you, Mary Karr, for all your support and care for my work. Without these people's effect on me during my time in Syracuse, surviving that space would have been an unlikely task.

Thank you to my cohort at Tin House: Alonso, Michelle, Meg, Jessica, and Caitlin. The tremendous help I received from y'all at Newport and beyond has been such a huge help to me as a poet. And the biggest thank you to our workshop leader, Solmaz Sharif. The way you forced me to confront the work and myself has changed me as a writer, and I will continue learning from your advice and your particular kind of grace you offer to the world.

Thank you to my amazing friends from the Juniper Conference: Vanessa, Nicholas, Manuel, and stevie. And to my poetry friends from all over: C.R., Patryja, Joy, and Randall.

Thank you to my family: my parents, my siblings, and Kayla. And the biggest thank you to my daughter, Ozara, who I love above all. And thank you to my friends: Nha, Viet, David, Raman, Ratan, Josh, and Chan.

WISCONSIN POETRY SERIES

Sean Bishop and Jesse Lee Kercheval, series editors
Ronald Wallace, founding series editor

How the End First Showed (B) • D. M. Aderibigbe

New Jersey (B) • Betsy Andrews

Salt (B) • Renée Ashley

Horizon Note (B) • Robin Behn

About Crows (FP) • Craig Blais

Mrs. Dumpty (FP) • Chana Bloch

Shopping, or The End of Time (FP) • Emily Bludworth de Barrios

The Declarable Future (4L) • Jennifer Boyden

The Mouths of Grazing Things (B) • Jennifer Boyden

Help Is on the Way (4L) • John Brehm

No Day at the Beach • John Brehm

Sea of Faith (B) • John Brehm

Reunion (FP) • Fleda Brown

Brief Landing on the Earth's Surface (B) • Juanita Brunk

Ejo: Poems, Rwanda, 1991–1994 (FP) • Derick Burleson

Grace Engine • Joshua Burton

Jagged with Love (B) • Susanna Childress

Almost Nothing to Be Scared Of (4L) • David Clewell

The Low End of Higher Things • David Clewell

Now We're Getting Somewhere (FP) • David Clewell

Taken Somehow by Surprise (4L) • David Clewell

Thunderhead • Emily Rose Cole

Borrowed Dress (FP) • Cathy Colman

(B) = Winner of the Brittingham Prize in Poetry
(FP) = Winner of the Felix Pollak Prize in Poetry
(4L) = Winner of the Four Lakes Prize in Poetry

Dear Terror, Dear Splendor • Melissa Crowe

Places/Everyone (B) • Jim Daniels

Show and Tell • Jim Daniels

Darkroom (B) • Jazzy Danziger

And Her Soul Out of Nothing (B) • Olena Kalytiak Davis

My Favorite Tyrants (B) • Joanne Diaz

Midwhistle • Dante Di Stefano

Talking to Strangers (B) • Patricia Dobler

Alien Miss • Carlina Duan

The Golden Coin (4L) • Alan Feldman

Immortality (4L) • Alan Feldman

A Sail to Great Island (FP) • Alan Feldman

The Word We Used for It (B) • Max Garland

A Field Guide to the Heavens (B) • Frank X. Gaspar

The Royal Baker's Daughter (FP) • Barbara Goldberg

Fractures (FP) • Carlos Andrés Gómez

Gloss • Rebecca Hazelton

Funny (FP) • Jennifer Michael Hecht

Queen in Blue • Ambalila Hemsell

The Legend of Light (FP) • Bob Hicok

Sweet Ruin (B) • Tony Hoagland

Partially Excited States (FP) • Charles Hood

Ripe (FP) • Roy Jacobstein

Last Seen (FP) • Jacqueline Jones LaMon

Perigee (B) • Diane Kerr

American Parables (B) • Daniel Khalastchi

Saving the Young Men of Vienna (B) • David Kirby

Conditions of the Wounded • Anna Leigh Knowles

Ganbatte (FP) • Sarah Kortemeier

Falling Brick Kills Local Man (FP) •Mark Kraushaar